LYNDON B. JOHNSON

OTHER BOOKS BY LOUANN ATKINS TEMPLE IN THE BIOGRAPHY FOR BEGINNING HISTORIANS SERIES

Barbara Bush

George W. Bush

Laura Bush

George H. W. Bush

Lady Bird Johnson

LYNDON B. JOHNSON

A Biography for Beginning Historians

LOUANN ATKINS TEMPLE

THE LBJ FOUNDATION

Distributed by the University of Texas Press

First LBJ Foundation Edition, 2025

♾ The paper used in this book meets the minimum requirements of ANSI/NISO Z39.48-1992 (R1997) (Permanence of Paper).

Library of Congress Control Number: 2025937833

ISBN 978-1-4773-3214-6 (paperback)
ISBN 978-1-4773-3215-3 (PDF)
ISBN 978-1-4773-3216-0 (ePub)

doi:10.7560/332146

To
Annie, Andy, Taylor, John, and Will—
I wrote this for you.

He was marvelous, contradictory, with a great natural intelligence . . . sometimes hurtful, but also sweet and caring and giving. . . . He valued my judgment, and I think sometimes I might have been helpful. I know we were better together than apart.

—LADY BIRD JOHNSON

CONTENTS

LYNDON B. JOHNSON

INTRODUCTION

When Lyndon Johnson, one of the most productive presidents in American history, said, "He's a can-do man" or "She's a can-do woman," he was offering his highest praise. He meant that he admired that person for setting out to do a job and doing it well. This man Lyndon Johnson, himself a whirlwind of a president, worked harder than most people and achieved stunning success in much of what he tried. He matched his can-do spirit with compassion for the people of his country who needed more education or better jobs or safer neighborhoods or who lacked good food and housing or who were discriminated against because of the color of their skin.

A can-do spirit, however, was not enough to allow him to accomplish all he wanted to as president because he governed during a time of change and conflict in his country. Young people were experimenting with new ways to dress and look and behave. Many young men wore long hair instead of cropping it close to their heads; many young women stopped wearing a skirt and matching sweater set with a string of pearls and instead put on blue jeans and a T-shirt. Rather than obeying adults unquestioningly, they began to say, "We don't like your fighting a war, and we don't like your telling women they can't have the same jobs as men, and we don't like your telling people of other races that they aren't allowed to have the same opportunities as white people." The changes they sought, however, did not come about easily or quickly. All of America joined in a loud conversation as they argued back and forth about making new rules for their lives. The president wanted to encourage good change, but he also wanted to keep the country safe and orderly. Sometimes people quit talking and carrying signs of protest and started rioting—throwing things and hurting one another. Sometimes, those who objected to the protests also let their anger get out of control. Sometimes, as a result, the president had to bring in soldiers to maintain order. His job was to keep his country peaceful while allowing its citizens to talk about their problems in a way that was good for the country and not destructive.

Being a can-do person, however, is not only about succeeding. It is also about continuing to try against tough odds. You are about to read a story of a man who, in angry, troubled times, never quit trying to solve his country's problems and never gave up on his dream of making it a better place for all its citizens. *That's* a can-do man.

CHAPTER 1
CHILDHOOD

Lyndon Baines Johnson, from Texas, became the thirty-sixth president of the United States in 1963. Americans called him LBJ. This Texas cowboy–looking man stood six feet three inches tall and wore a Stetson hat. He combed his hair straight back from his face, which was lined and sunbrowned from growing up on a farm. When he talked to people, he stood close to them and looked deep into their eyes, often trying with words and his oversize presence to persuade them to join him in action. He paid close and serious attention to all that he did, and he had the energy and curiosity to do much. When he was not working, he did not like to be alone; he wanted his family and friends around him all the time for fast-moving conversation and for trading jokes and good stories.

When LBJ became president in 1963, Americans lived much as they do today. In 1908, when he was born, however, people lived more like pioneers. He lived in one of the most remote and poorest parts of the country. That hardship gave him a fierce drive to accomplish other things. Television and commercial airplanes did not exist. On the farms near Stonewall, Texas, where he was born, no one had electric lights or dishwashers or even indoor toilets or bathtubs and sinks with running water. They owned no telephones or cars. The Johnsons worked hard on their farm. Lyndon's father, Sam, plowed fields, slopped hogs, chopped wood, and hauled dozens of buckets of water into the house for bathing and cleaning and cooking. His mother, Rebekah, fed chickens, grew vegetables, sewed the family's clothes, cooked in a fireplace, and scrubbed the floor on her hands and knees. Chores on a farm never ended.

When baby Lyndon arrived, on August 27, 1908, his proud father rode his horse Fritz to the houses of nearby family and friends to announce the news. Lyndon's mother was equally thrilled; she was not used to the work of a farmer's wife, and the birth of her first son made her hard life on a farm seem worthwhile. Before her marriage, she had lived in town, had graduated from Baylor University, had taught public speaking, and had reported for the newspaper. Both her college education and her working at a paid job were highly unusual for a young woman at that time.

Two years after Lyndon's birth, he had a little sister. Every two years after that another Johnson baby was born, until there were five: Lyndon, Rebekah, Josefa, Sam Houston, and Lucia.

Lyndon stayed close to his mother as a small child and to his father as he got older. He said that his mother "kept me constantly amused. I remember playing games with her that only the two of us could play." Another time he remembered, "She needed me to take care of her. It made me believe I could do anything in the whole world." Rebekah saw how bright her little boy was and taught him to read and to recite poetry long before he was old enough to attend school. She loved to read grown-up books to him, like the poetry of John

Lyndon Baines Johnson (LBJ) near his home in Johnson City, Texas, around 1915. Courtesy of the LBJ Presidential Library and Museum.

Milton and the novels of Charles Dickens, and she told him stories from the Bible and history and mythology and about her own childhood.

When he was four or five years old, Lyndon's parents had a disagreement. His hair was long and hung in ringlets, which his mother thought were beautiful. His father, though, said, "You're making a sissy of him." While his mother was at church one day, his father cut off his curls. Rebekah Johnson did not speak to her husband for a week.

About this time, the Johnson family left the farm and moved to Johnson City, a town of 323 people, where young Lyndon's father went into the real estate business and his mother taught debate at the local high school. When business was not good for Sam Johnson, they returned for a few years to farm life. While they lived on the farm, young Lyndon rode a donkey to school; there, about sixty children of all ages learned together in one room.

The Johnson children did chores, but the younger brother and sisters remembered that Lyndon didn't work as much as they did; he was bossy, telling them what to do. Sometimes, if they resisted, he bribed them with cookies. His brother Sam Houston, six years younger, remembered that at other times Lyndon was protective of him and that he taught him how to play dominoes and to ride a bike.

At school, Lyndon often got in trouble for playing practical jokes, acting like a clown, and not doing his homework. He found it hard to sit still to do his work, but his mother was determined he should. She would ask him in the morning if his lessons were prepared. If they were not, she read them to him during breakfast and even walked to school with him, continuing to read aloud, until the studying was completed.

LBJ (*second from right*) with his brother and three younger sisters, around 1921. Courtesy of the LBJ Presidential Library and Museum.

Not only was Lyndon's father a farmer and a real estate man, but he also was elected as a legislator, helping to pass laws for the state of Texas. By the time Lyndon was ten years old, he had discovered something he did love to study—his father's world of politics. He thrilled to go with him to the Capitol building in Austin, where he listened for hours as the legislators discussed the state's business. Often he wandered the halls of the Capitol, trying to figure out what this world of government was all about. In election years he proudly traveled with his father to the towns in the Central Texas Hill Country, listening to him make speeches explaining why people should vote for him to represent them in the legislature. More and more at night he hung around near the porch just to watch his father and his father's friends drink beer and play dominoes and talk about politics and tell jokes and swap stories. That remained one of Lyndon's favorite ways to spend an evening, even while he was president.

After he graduated from the eleventh grade (the last grade of high school at that time), fifteen-year-old Lyndon had no idea what he wanted to do with his life. His parents thought he should go to college, and he later said, "I think except for [my mother] I might not have made it through high school and certainly not through college." He decided, instead, to drive to California with several friends to experience living in another part of the United States. Because he was afraid to tell his family that he was not obeying their wishes, he sneaked out of the house one morning and was off on his first independent adventure. His angry father, after learning what his son had done, called the sheriff of nearly every county between Johnson City and the New Mexico border, telling them to arrest Lyndon and send him back home, but the boys avoided being caught. Lyndon's mother reacted more sympathetically. She called his aunt in Fredericksburg, told her that Lyndon had forgotten to take a pillow with him, and asked her to please loan him one if he stopped at her house. However, the boy on the run did not stop at his aunt's house.

The friends drove ten days to reach California, getting lost along the way and making a side trip to see the Grand Canyon. Because they didn't have much money, they camped out rather than stayed in hotels. What little money they had they buried each time they rested, and one of them slept on top of the loose dirt lest they be robbed. At one stop they had to shoot a rattlesnake before they could lie down to sleep.

The boys arrived in California with only eight dollars. Fortunately, Lyndon had a cousin in San Bernardino he could stay with while he looked for a job. The work he found was meager: washing dishes, waiting tables, herding goats, and running errands for a law office.

Finally, discouraged and homesick, he went back to Texas. His parents again argued and pleaded with him to go to college, but he again refused. He found a job laboring on a construction crew building a highway. Working in the hot Texas sun with his hands was hard and unsatisfying. Slowly, on his own, he began to realize that his high school education was not enough learning to get him the kind of life he wanted. Thinking he might like to become a teacher, he enrolled in Southwest Texas State Teacher's College, in San Marcos, fifty miles from home.

That first year in college, Lyndon was homesick, as he had been in California, and he struggled academically and financially. But he was determined to stay. He studied history and education. He disliked physical education, and he made his lowest grade in PE. By this time, he was tall and thin and had wavy black hair. He walked fast and talked fast, and he seemed as if he were always in a hurry to get somewhere. Like his father, he was friendly and talked to anyone he saw. He especially enjoyed discussing politics, and he loved telling stories to amuse his friends. All his life, he was a good storyteller.

Lyndon lacked money for college, so he worked after class each day to pay for his education. His jobs as a janitor and a door-to-door salesman did not entirely cover classes, food, and a room to live in, however, so he left school to earn the money he needed. Today teachers must graduate from

LBJ (*center*) with his fifth, sixth, and seventh grade classes at Welhausen School, Cotulla, Texas, 1928. Courtesy of the LBJ Presidential Library and Museum.

college before beginning their career, but in 1928 the rules were not as strict. He got a job as a teacher of fifth, sixth, and seventh graders in the hot, dusty little town of Cotulla, Texas. The temperature in Cotulla could rise to 110 degrees. There were no shady trees to stand under. Most of his students were much poorer than he had ever been. After he became president, many years later, he would remember these children and their parents. He wanted them to have easier lives and fewer struggles. As president, he tried to make laws to help people like his students.

Twenty-year-old Lyndon taught in Cotulla and saved his money until he had enough to return to San Marcos and finish college. Finally, with a diploma in hand, he was ready for the adult world. He thought about the kind of person he had become. He never tired of working. He was happiest when talking to people and solving problems. He wanted to help those whose lives were difficult. He cared about history. He especially loved the workings of government, which he had learned from watching his father. He wanted to be a leader. He knew that politics was the right career for him.

CHAPTER 2

GOING TO WASHINGTON

Like many young people at the start of their careers, Lyndon Johnson was not sure how to begin. While he was trying to learn more about politics, he returned to teaching, this time at a Houston high school. He remained interested in politics and government, so in the evenings, after work, he volunteered to help a Texan named Richard Kleberg in his campaign to be elected to Congress. Congress members represent their neighbors in Washington, DC, just as Lyndon's father had represented his neighbors in Austin in the Texas legislature. When Kleberg won the election, he offered twenty-three-year-old Lyndon a job running his office in Washington. LBJ's career in politics, which would last a lifetime, had now begun.

He worked seven days a week at his new job, beginning at seven o'clock in the morning and often ending as late as midnight, and he expected everyone around him to work hard also. He sent part of his salary home each month to help his parents.

The first thing Lyndon learned about politics was that he needed to meet as many people as possible who worked in government. He lived in a building with many other young men who were congressional aides, and he tried to get to know them all. He made a plan. They all shared a large bathroom, and when he first arrived, he took four showers one night and brushed his teeth five different times the next morning. He knew that the other aides would come in to shower and brush their teeth, and that if he stayed in the bathroom long enough, he would meet everyone. He looked for other ways to happen across government workers who did not live in his building.

The second thing he learned about politics was the importance of knowing the people back in Texas who voted. When the time came for the next election, he traveled back and forth across the part of the state Kleberg represented, meeting hundreds of people and telling them about his boss.

Lyndon was now twenty-six years old. One day in Austin, a friend introduced him to a young woman who had recently graduated from the University of Texas. Her name was Claudia Taylor, but everyone called her Lady Bird. She remembered later that being with Lyndon "was just like finding yourself in the middle of a whirlwind" because, on their first date, he told her so much about his family, his job, and his dreams for his life, and he peppered her with questions about herself. They began that first date with breakfast at the Driskill Hotel. Then they drove around Austin and into the nearby hills, talking, all day long. Before the end of the day, he asked her to marry him. Shocked, she replied, "You must be joking." Nevertheless, he continued to propose again and again, and ten weeks later she married this man whom she called "the most outspoken, straightforward, determined person I'd ever encountered." Without telling their families, they drove to San Antonio, and in a lavender dress, at eight o'clock at night, Lady Bird wed Lyndon at St. Mark's Episcopal Church.

Afterward, with twelve friends, they dined and danced at the St. Anthony Hotel and began a life together that lasted until Lyndon Johnson's death thirty-eight years later.

The young woman who married Lyndon Johnson became the anchor in his life. She matched his restless charging ahead to get things done with her own ever-patient and calm judgment and a softness he needed at the end of a hurly-burly day. Lady Bird grew up in East Texas, in a more Southern and graceful world than the hardscrabble Hill Country that Lyndon had known. Her mother had died when she was five years old, and the little girl, though well cared for in a big house, learned about solitude at an early age. As a child, she walked in the woods and the flower-strewn fields near her home in Karnack, Texas, and there she developed a deep love of nature. She did well in school and went on to college, graduating at a time when more young men than young women attended college.

Lyndon became restless at his job running a congressional office. He dreamed of being a congress member himself. He noticed that many politicians were lawyers, so he went to law school at night for a short time. He quit because he felt that the school was not adequately teaching him practical ways to solve problems.

Then he found a job he wanted back in Texas. He applied to President Franklin Roosevelt for an appointment as director of the National Youth Administration in Austin. At first, President Roosevelt feared that at twenty-six, Lyndon was too young for the job, but he decided to give him a chance. The NYA helped young people finish school if they did not have money and to find jobs when jobs were scarce. Lyndon wanted every young person to be able to learn and to work

Newlyweds Lyndon and Lady Bird Johnson pose near the US Capitol, around 1934. Courtesy of the LBJ Presidential Library and Museum.

and to have the best life possible. He started the new youth program with his usual gusto, working his staff seven days a week, late into the night. He loved his job because he was helping people, but he worked so hard and got so little sleep that he often was sick with colds or the flu and several times had pneumonia. He did such a good job that Eleanor Roosevelt, the First Lady, traveled to Texas to observe how he was running the NYA so that she could pass on his ideas to other directors across the country. She and the president decided that, even though he was young himself, Lyndon Johnson knew how to help young people better than anyone else in the United States.

Finally, his chance came to run for office. The congressman from his district in Texas died. Lyndon had his heart set on running, but he would have to quit his job to do so, and he had no money. Lady Bird, who believed in her husband, made the first contribution to his campaign with $10,000, which she had inherited from her family. Eight other people announced for the same race, but Lyndon believed he could beat them all if he met enough voters. He drove throughout his district every day, talking and shaking hands. When he saw a farmer in the field, he climbed the fence and talked to him. When he drove by a service station, he bought a gallon of gasoline and met everyone at the station. He walked down the main street of small towns, stopping people to tell them who he was. After six weeks he was exhausted and sick with appendicitis. He spent the last few days of the campaign in the hospital, having his appendix removed. While he was recovering, he learned that he had been elected to Congress. His hard work had paid off. Lyndon and Lady Bird were moving back to Washington. This time, rather than working for a congressman from Texas, he would *be* a congressman from Texas.

CHAPTER 3

HOUSE OF REPRESENTATIVES

Lyndon Johnson had long recognized that he could learn from experienced men who were older than him. In Congress, he gained two mentors who helped him understand government and politics in all their complexity. One was President Franklin Roosevelt, who saw into the future when he said of LBJ, "This boy could well be the first Southern president." The other mentor was a fellow Texan named Sam Rayburn. Sam was the leader of the House of Representatives. His title was Speaker of the House. The two men worked together all week at the Capitol, and almost every Sunday Sam ate dinner with the Johnsons. They remained close friends throughout their lives.

Congressman Johnson continued his habits of working until he was exhausted and sick and pushing his staff equally hard. He insisted that they answer every letter from a voter back home the day it came into the office. Paying attention to the problems of the people who voted for you was what got you reelected, he told them. He also continued trying to know well all the congress members and government workers he dealt with. He raised money for many Democratic politicians in Congress who were facing elections they might

Recently elected Congressman Johnson (*right*) meets with President Franklin Roosevelt in Galveston, Texas, May 1937. Courtesy of the LBJ Presidential Library and Museum.

not otherwise win without some help. He employed a young Texan, John Connally, as his aide. John later became governor of Texas and ran for president himself.

One of Lyndon's proudest accomplishments as a congressman was that he helped get dams built across the rivers in Central Texas so that his neighbors in the country would have electricity. Their lives would be easier. One Texan remembers coming home after dark to see light inside her house for the first time. Such an unfamiliar sight made her fear that her house was on fire.

Congressman Johnson became restless again. He hoped to be a senator and to represent his entire state instead of a small section as he was doing now, and he wanted to be one of ninety-six senators rather than one of 435 representatives. An opponent beat him in the senate race, however—the colorful Governor of Texas W. Lee "Pappy" O'Daniel, who had been a hillbilly singer and whose motto was "Pass the Biscuits, Pappy," because he had sold flour before he was governor. Lyndon tried mightily; he had support from President Roosevelt, and he even hired a band himself to campaign with him. After the election, Lyndon Johnson was declared the winner until some uncounted votes came in that made O'Daniel the new senator by a little over a thousand votes. No doubt, the election had not been honest, but in those days election rules were not enforced strictly. Lyndon tried to hide his heartbreak. Shortly after the election, Lady Bird said, "His head was high, and he was stepping along real spryly. I know how much nerve and effort were now required for him to keep up that courageous appearance." He later described the days after the lost election as the most miserable in his life.

America by now had entered World War II, fighting the Germans in Europe and the Japanese across the Pacific Ocean. Congressman Johnson joined the Navy and went to the Pacific, while Mrs. Johnson ran his congressional office in Washington.

After her husband returned, Lady Bird Johnson, who had spent part of her inheritance to pay for LBJ's congressional campaign, now chose to invest more of it in a radio station in Austin called KTBC. For many years she worked to make KTBC a profitable radio station and, later, a successful television and radio business. People who worked with her appreciated her close attention to every little detail of how the station operated and how it spent its money. She often traveled between Washington, DC, and Austin, juggling her jobs as a businessperson and as a congressional wife.

In the next few years, the Johnsons' lives changed in important ways. Their first daughter, Lynda Bird, was born. President Roosevelt died, and Harry S. Truman became president. The war ended. Then a second daughter, Lucy Baines, arrived. When LBJ was forty years old he ran for the Senate a second time, even though he was afraid he would be beaten. He had been badly hurt when he lost before, but he decided that he wanted to be a senator so he must try again.

As a congressman, he had represented people only in Central Texas, but as a senator he would have to win the votes of a majority of all Texans. Once again he tried to meet as many voters as possible, but this time the job was more difficult because he would be covering the entire state instead of only one district. He decided he could meet the challenge by traveling in a helicopter, an aircraft rarely seen in those days. He flew to 118 towns in seventeen days, and the crowds flocked to this unusual sight. As his craft hovered in the air, he would shout over a loudspeaker, "Hello down there. This is Lyndon Johnson, your candidate for the US Senate." Then, after he landed and opened the helicopter's door, he would toss his Stetson hat into the crowd. People usually whooped and hollered in response, as if they were at a rodeo or a football game. While he shook their hands, his aides would have to hunt for the hat and sometimes pay a dollar to someone who had caught it in order to get it back.

When the race was over, Lyndon Johnson had defeated Governor Coke Stevenson by only eighty-seven votes. Both sides claimed that the other had played unfairly. People are still arguing the question.

CHAPTER 4

SENATE

In the Senate, Lyndon Johnson's big, exuberant personality, his intelligence, and his devotion to work came together to produce what many have called the most effective leader of the Senate in American history. To understand how he achieved such success, let us first see how he became the Senate's leader.

He did the four things he had done in every new job. First, he found a mentor—Senator Richard Russell from Georgia, who instructed him on the workings of the Senate and who became his lifelong friend. Lyndon Johnson was looking for someone to teach him and to help him solve problems by talking them over. He and Senator Russell spent their weekdays at work and their weekends at the Johnsons' home together. Second, the new Senator Johnson studied avidly how to do his job. He felt he must learn everything about the problems that he would vote on for the country and must understand the rules of the Senate. He was thirsty for information and could never get enough. Third, he set out to know well the people he worked with, from how they felt about bills before the Congress to the names of their children. Fourth, he worked harder than anyone else. Sometimes he would work around the clock, napping a few hours in his office and asking Lady Bird to bring him fresh clothes from home in the morning.

His devotion catapulted him to head of the Senate within a few years. The party that contains more than half the members of the Senate is called the majority party. Its powerful leader is named the Majority Leader. The party with fewer members is known as the minority party, and its leader is called the Minority Leader. When Lyndon Johnson first went to the Senate, the Democrats were the minority party. Within four years they had named him their Minority Leader. The next year, they became the majority party. They chose LBJ as Majority Leader.

He thought it was important in this job for Democrats and Republicans to work well with each other and for the Senate to work well with President Dwight David Eisenhower, who was a Republican. LBJ promoted bipartisanship, which means Republicans and Democrats trying to find ways to agree so that they could pass laws satisfactory to both. Regularly, the two Democrats—Majority Leader Lyndon Johnson and Speaker of the House Sam Rayburn—met secretly with Republican President Dwight Eisenhower at the White House and talked about ways the two political parties could help the country together. When asked about this unusual cooperation between leaders of opposing parties, Senator Johnson said of President Eisenhower, "If you're in an airplane, and you're flying somewhere, you don't run up to the cockpit and attack the pilot. Mr. Eisenhower is the only president we've got." When Senator Johnson became president, he met in the same way with Republican leader Senator Everett Dirksen. These four patriots from different political par-

President Dwight Eisenhower and Senator Johnson share a laugh at the White House, around 1955. Courtesy of the LBJ Presidential Library and Museum.

ties each wanted his team to win elections against the other, but they all wanted the country to be the final winner by having good laws both sides could support.

He tried to make other senators' jobs easier for them. Whether they were Democrats or Republicans, he saw to it that each got to work on a committee studying problems that really interested that person. He never asked a senator to vote in a way to make the people from his home state angry. He tried to make senators his friends by doing nice things for them: helping one to find an office employee, asking another to represent the Senate at a conference in Europe, sending congratulations on birthdays and wedding anniversaries.

He also used what became known as "the Treatment" to persuade people to vote with him. When he wanted something from another person, he would tower over him with their noses almost touching and overwhelm him with pleas and arguments and statistics and his booming, hypnotizing personality until that person simply wilted in the face of so much energy directed at him from such close range. One newspaperman said it was "as if a St. Bernard had licked your face for an hour, had pawed you all over." That was the Treatment. It was very dramatic.

It was during the Senate years that Lyndon and Lady Bird bought from his aunt and uncle their ranch, where Lyndon remembered spending happy Christmases and summer holidays as a child in Texas. This land was hilly and rocky; it was peppered with cattle and deer and live oak and pecan trees and rivers and creeks that flooded one year and struggled to stay moist the next, and it fed him as surely as food. As he rose in power and responsibility within the government, he found it necessary to his well-being to return there often, where he said the land and the people refreshed and inspired him as nothing else could. Lady Bird simply said, "It is our heart's home."

People were suggesting that Lyndon Johnson should be president of the United States until a serious problem stopped him in his tracks. When he was forty-six years old, he suffered a heart attack. After he left the hospital, many months passed before he could work again.

When he did return to the Senate, the important question of segregation faced the country. Black Americans had begun objecting strenuously to segregation. In many states there were laws that said they could not sit side by side with white riders on buses and trains and that they must use separate restrooms and water fountains and go to different schools from white children. This was called the civil rights issue. LBJ, all his life, had hated that his part of the country believed in segregation. He believed passionately that everyone should have equal opportunity to secure good jobs, any seat on the bus, and admission to the same schools. The beginnings of discussion about this most serious problem in America, as well as the first small steps toward passing laws to make Black and white citizens full partners, began at this time. After Johnson became president, more laws would help make Black rights a reality.

Then Russia shocked Americans by launching a man into space in a satellite called *Sputnik*. Americans already feared the power of Russia, a country then unfriendly to the United States. Lyndon Johnson was at his Texas ranch when he heard the news. He walked outside and stared at the sky in amazement, both at the wonder of humans conquering space and at the fact that another nation, especially such an intimidating one, would be the one to do so first. He became the leader in convincing Americans that we, too, could soar in space and that we must. He saw to it that a law was passed creating NASA, the National Aeronautics and Space Administration, to help America surpass Russia in space exploration.

Since his graduation from college, Lyndon Johnson had been a schoolteacher, an aide to a congressman, a congressman himself, and a senator. Next, he would become vice president of the United States.

CHAPTER 5

THE VICE PRESIDENCY

In 1960 the Democrats chose John Fitzgerald Kennedy as their candidate for president, and John Kennedy asked Lyndon Johnson to be his running mate as vice president. The two men were elected, but soon Lyndon realized that he disliked being vice president. He no longer was in a position to make decisions for his country. He could only stand by and watch others make those important choices. He had thrived on being a leader, and now he was reduced to being an assistant to someone else's leadership.

Representing the president, he spent much of his time flying to other countries, telling people about democracy in America. As vice president, he traveled to thirty-three countries, where he mostly shook hands and made speeches when what he longed to do was solve problems. A meeting with an unexpected outcome occurred while the vice president was in Pakistan. Lyndon saw a man standing beside his camel along the side of a road. He shook the surprised man's hand and said casually, "Y'all come to Washington and see us sometime." To the vice president's astonishment, the camel-driver took him seriously and accepted. Rather than back down on an invitation he had meant to be friendly but not real, Lyn-

Vice President Johnson visits with President John Kennedy in the Oval Office, 1963. Courtesy of the LBJ Presidential Library and Museum.

don brought the camel-driver, who spoke no English, back to the United States and entertained him in Texas, Washington, DC, and New York while the world watched on television, delighted with this impromptu bit of foreign diplomacy.

Back home, Vice President Johnson concentrated on the space program. He met with scientists and with military and political and business leaders on the problems of space travel. Then he reported to the president that, although it would be very expensive, America should send a man to the moon, and shortly after he left the presidency, America did land astronauts on the moon. It was a proud day for the United States.

He also continued while he was vice president to devote

his time to helping Black Americans. He and President Kennedy knew it was wrong that Black people were not given a fair chance to get jobs, that they often were not allowed to vote in elections, and that they could not use the same restrooms and water fountains and seats on buses and trains as white Americans. Many white people, especially in the South, where the majority of Black citizens lived, were so used to these rules that they saw no need to change them. Lyndon felt angry and frustrated that many people would not listen to him when he tried to convince them that this was unfair.

Finally, the vice president's job was made difficult by the fact that he and President Kennedy's brother Bobby Kennedy did not like each other. Bobby Kennedy was attorney general, the lawyer for the country. The two men had to work together often, and neither was happy about it.

On November 22, 1963, a terrible thing happened. President Kennedy and Vice President Johnson and their wives had gone on a short trip to Texas so that the president could raise money for his upcoming reelection campaign. In Dallas, shortly after noon, they were driving slowly through the city streets in open-topped cars, waving to welcoming crowds. The day was sunny; people from Dallas were excited to have a president in their city. Suddenly, a gun fired. From the sixth floor of a building along the parade route, a man named Lee Harvey Oswald had shot President Kennedy. In the car in which Lyndon and Lady Bird Johnson were riding, a brave Secret Service agent named Rufus Youngblood was sitting in the front seat while the Johnsons were in the back. He heard the shots. "Get down! Get down!" he yelled to the vice president as he leaped over the front seat and threw his own body on top of Lyndon to protect him from harm.

Shortly after President Kennedy's assassination, flanked by Lady Bird Johnson (*left*) and Kennedy's widow, Jacqueline, President Johnson is sworn into office aboard *Air Force One*, Dallas, Texas, November 1963. Courtesy of the LBJ Presidential Library and Museum.

The car sped behind President Kennedy's car to the hospital, where the Johnsons soon learned that the president had died. That same afternoon they, along with Mrs. Kennedy and a casket carrying President Kennedy's body, boarded the presidential airplane, called *Air Force One*. Inside the airplane, Lyndon Johnson, only about two hours after the president's death, was sworn in as the thirty-sixth president of the United States. By evening, President Johnson was back in Washington, working into the night at his new job to be sure the world knew that the United States still had a leader to guide it. Before he went to bed that night he wrote a note to each of President Kennedy's two young children, Caroline and John, to tell them how sad their father's death had made him.

A few days later, the sorrowful new president went to the Capitol and, in a speech before Congress, said, "All I have I would have given gladly not to be standing here today."

CHAPTER 6

THE GREAT SOCIETY

Lyndon Johnson imagined an America that he called "the Great Society." In the Great Society, poor people would be helped to find jobs, old people would receive health care even if they could not pay for it, and any child who had the ability could go to college. Theaters and orchestras and operas would be enjoyed, not just in a few big cities, but across the country and on television. The air and water around us would be kept clean and pure, and new national parks would be established. Most importantly, in the Great Society, hotels and restaurants and playgrounds and houses and apartments would no longer be for "Whites Only," as signs outside their doors sometimes read, and Black citizens would vote as freely as white citizens. All Americans would share the good things in their country in ways they never had before.

When he became president unexpectedly, Lyndon Johnson went to work energetically to make these dreams come true. He appointed fourteen different committees to come up with ideas of how to make the country even better, and then he presented many of their suggestions to Congress. Some feared that these new projects would be too expensive, and some believed they would encourage the government to interfere too much in people's lives. His plans, however, were agreed to by a majority in Congress, and they were passed into law and have made the lives of millions of Americans safer, longer, and more productive.

For civil rights, the new laws said no one could be refused a job or kept out of a public place because of the color of their skin; no state could keep poor people from casting a ballot by charging them a tax as the price of voting; and no one could be denied a place to live because of their race. The two leaders to remember in the all-important civil rights movement are Lyndon Johnson and Martin Luther King, each contributing what he did best. President Johnson forced the passage of laws by persuading enough congress members to vote for them at a time when many did not want to and by never giving up until the job was done. Dr. Martin Luther King, a Black minister from Georgia, inspired Black Americans to insist on their rights and to be unafraid of people who threatened them. He made stirring speeches to keep their spirits and courage up, and he led marches on public streets to show people how strongly they felt and how many of them they were. The two men, Johnson and King, met in the White House to discuss their plans.

For education, money from Washington was given to schools for the first time. The money helped young people of all ages whose families did not make much money. A program called Head Start offered nursery school and kindergarten classes. Money for older children was used to purchase classroom materials, to help pay for special education, and to teach students in their native language if they could not speak English. College-age young people who needed financial help were offered scholarships and loans.

Two weeks after becoming president, President Johnson meets with Dr. Martin Luther King Jr. in the Oval Office, beginning their close partnership on civil rights, December 1963. Courtesy of the LBJ Presidential Library and Museum.

Because he had never forgotten the poor people he had known when he had taught school in Cotulla as a young man, President Johnson began a program called the War on Poverty. It started the Job Corps, which helped train young people so they could get employment.

Because of his concern for the health problems of older Americans, he established Medicare, which helped people pay for medical services in the last years of their lives.

President Johnson signs the Immigration and Nationality Act near the Statue of Liberty, Liberty Island, New York, October 1965. Courtesy of the LBJ Presidential Library and Museum.

He started the National Endowment for the Arts and the National Endowment for the Humanities and the public broadcasting system, all of which made clear that because the arts and learning were important in people's lives, they should be supported by the government.

He cared about the environment. During his presidency, thirty-five new national parks were established, as well as thousands of miles of hiking trails. Lady Bird contributed also, in ways that expressed her own love of nature and her concern for protecting it. She was behind a law that limited billboards and hid junkyards along the sides of highways. She tried to make Washington a model city the rest of the country could copy by beautifying Pennsylvania Avenue, which ran from the White House to the Capitol; by creating parks throughout the city; by planting gardens full of daffodils and pink dogwood trees like she had known in East Texas; and by cleaning up poor neighborhoods. She also took forty strenuous trips into wilderness areas to make the public aware of the treasure they were for the country.

In the midst of all this bill passing, President Johnson had to run for reelection. Senator Hubert Humphrey of Minnesota was his running mate as vice president. Lyndon Johnson won the majority vote in forty-four of the fifty states, and more people voted for him than had ever voted for a president before. In a few years, however, he would be a very unpopular president because of the war in Vietnam.

CHAPTER 7

THE VIETNAM WAR

One terrible problem overwhelmed Lyndon Johnson's presidency: communism in a country called Vietnam, nearly ten thousand miles away.

Communism intends for everyone to own everything together so that no one person has more possessions than another. Its government divides up what the people have, and it tells people what they must do without and where they must live and work. In China, the Communist government even controls how many children they may have. That government is not elected, so it cannot be overturned if the people disagree with its decisions. Citizens are not allowed to complain.

When Lyndon Johnson was president, communism was on the move throughout the world. The Communists openly scorned American democracy, and they tried to persuade other countries to become communist. America treasured its freedom for people to choose how they wanted to live, and they loved its elections, in which they picked their own government instead of having one forced on them. They feared the Communists' victories in other parts of the world.

Two huge countries—Russia and China—had already

turned to communism. A small country, Vietnam, which was right next to China, was struggling to decide which form of government it would choose. The Communist North Vietnam was fighting the Democratic South Vietnam. Many people in America believed that if all of Vietnam became communist, it would persuade other countries to do the same. The fall of each country to communism would make another country fall, in turn, like lined-up dominoes, until there was no place left for democracy. This view is known as the Domino Theory.

At first, the United States sent members of the military to Vietnam to teach the Democratic South Vietnamese how to fight the Communist North Vietnamese. The Americans themselves did not fight. They only advised. Then, one Sunday morning, three North Vietnamese torpedo boats attacked an American ship called the USS *Maddox*, which was lying sixteen miles off the shore of Vietnam. The *Maddox* fought back, sinking one of the torpedo boats. Later, North Vietnam attacked some US military advisers, killing eight of them, and again America made an attack of its own in response. Soon, the Americans and the South Vietnamese were fighting side by side against the North Vietnamese. Most Americans thought the president had made the right decision to fight. As time went by, however, many Americans began to believe that the war could not be won and that no US soldier should die over a small country on the other side of the world. No one knew what the future would hold, whether the country continued to fight in Vietnam or whether it left Vietnam.

Those who thought the war had to be fought were called hawks, and those who believed that the war was wrong were

President Johnson greets soldiers in Vietnam, October 1966.
Courtesy of the LBJ Presidential Library and Museum.

called doves. An argument raged between the two groups. Many families were torn between parents and children who disagreed. Those who protested the war held rallies, and thousands of people showed up. Those who supported the war called the protesters unpatriotic, and fights sometimes broke out. Every day, people marched outside the White House, shouting against the war, and whenever the president went out in public, they lined up to shout at him. One particularly harsh slogan chanted as he passed by was, "Hey, hey, LBJ, how many boys did you kill today?" Police held them back. Sometimes, young men who were told they must be drafted into the army ran away to another country rather than fight. America was not at peace with itself.

President Johnson was torn between thinking the war against communism must be won and not being sure it was possible to win. LBJ was so conflicted about the war that he remarked to National Security Adviser McGeorge Bundy, "I don't think it's worth fighting for, and I don't think we can get out. And it's just the biggest damn mess I ever saw."

It came time for the president once again to run for election. More and more Americans had turned against the war. This man the president, who understood politics so well, realized that he had lost the backing of the country. He could see that the war had reached a stalemate: No matter how many troops the US sent into Vietnam, the Communists continued to send more, and there seemed no end in sight. He feared that his health would not allow him to serve another term in office. He counted the cost of the war in lives lost and money and attention diverted from solving America's problems at

President Johnson's announcement about whether he will run for reelection, March 1968. Courtesy of the LBJ Presidential Library and Museum.

home. He decided, after struggling with the decision for months, that nothing was more important—not even being elected president of the United States—than to spend all his waking hours searching for an honorable end to a war that he and all other Americans hated. He must not, at the same time, conduct a backbreaking campaign for office that would drain his energies and further divide the American people.

And so, on March 31, 1968, Lyndon Johnson went on national television and said to a shocked audience, "With America's sons in the fields far away, with America's future under challenge right here at home, with our hopes and the world's hopes for peace in the balance every day, I do not believe that I should devote an hour or a day of my time to any personal partisan causes or to any duties other than the awesome duties of this office—the presidency of your country. Accordingly, I shall not seek, and I will not accept, the nomination of my party for another term as your president."

Ten months later, Republican Richard Nixon took his place in the White House as the thirty-seventh president, and Lady Bird and Lyndon went home to Texas and to retirement.

CHAPTER 8

THE END OF A LIFE OF SERVICE

On Monday morning, January 20, 1969, Lyndon and Lady Bird Johnson watched as President Nixon was sworn in on the Capitol grounds as the new president of the United States. At a farewell lunch, the Johnsons sadly said goodbye to the friends they had made during the many years they had lived in Washington. Then they helicoptered to Andrews Air Force Base, where the presidential plane waited to fly them one last time to Texas. When they landed at Bergstrom Air Force Base, in Austin, five thousand Texans welcomed them with banners and bouquets of flowers. The University of Texas Longhorn Band played "The Eyes of Texas." Finally, they took one last flight in a smaller plane to the LBJ ranch, arriving just at dark. Thirty-two years of public service in Washington lay behind them, and they had come home to their beloved Hill Country to stay.

For the next four years, the former president embraced life as energetically and passionately as ever. He oversaw the construction of a library and school in his name on the University of Texas campus. He wrote a book about his presidency. He saw to it that a nursing home named after his mother was built in Austin as an example of how to care for

Former President Johnson on his beloved LBJ Ranch, four months before his death, September 1972. Courtesy of the LBJ Presidential Library and Museum.

old people properly. He watched over his ranch, seeing that the cattle were tended and the fences were mended. He often invited friends to visit. He liked to drive them about the ranch before dinner, pointing out the white-tailed deer. Later in the evening, he and his guests often sat on lawn chairs in the front yard under a huge live oak tree, trading stories about politics and growing up in the Hill Country. Sometimes they played dominoes, just as his father and his friends had done over fifty years earlier. He let his hair, now white where it had once been black, grow to his shoulders. The immensity of the problems he had faced as president showed on his face; he looked much older than he was. He began to have heart trouble again. Four years after he returned to Texas—on January 22, 1973—Lyndon Johnson's heart stopped beating. Following a funeral in Washington, DC, the sixty-four-year-old president's body was returned to the Texas Hill Country he loved, and on a bitterly cold and rainy winter day, he was buried in the family cemetery within sight of the house in which he had been born, alongside his parents and his brother and sisters. Thirty-four years later, Lady Bird was laid to rest beside him.

Just a month before his death, President Johnson had thrilled to one last proud occasion, when hundreds of men and women interested in the civil rights movement came to the LBJ Library, in Austin, to discuss how Black and white Americans could continue to work toward equal opportunities for everyone. He told them, "The progress has been much too small. We haven't done nearly enough." The can-do president, even in illness, wanted to work harder and do more until all Americans, in his words, "stand on level and equal ground." That was Lyndon Johnson's dream.

Military officers carry former President Johnson's casket up the stairs of the Great Hall of the LBJ Presidential Library and Museum, January 1973. Courtesy of the LBJ Presidential Library and Museum.

His other dream—for every child to get "as much education as he has the ability to take"—was honored in 2007, thirty-four years after his death, when Congress voted to rename the Education Building in Washington, DC, to the Lyndon Baines Johnson Department of Education Building. This was a fitting tribute to the president who had passed sixty-six education laws and who was proud that he had once been a teacher himself.

With his can-do spirit, Lyndon Johnson had changed America. Although his hope for a world safe from communism had brought pain to the nation and to him, he did get to see his country become more welcoming to people of all races and more concerned with young people's education. Those are the two accomplishments for which he would have liked to be remembered.

SELECTED BIBLIOGRAPHY

Dallek, Robert. *Lyndon B. Johnson: Portrait of a President.* Oxford University Press, 2004.

Divine, Robert, ed. *Exploring the Johnson Years.* University of Texas Press, 1981.

First Lady Lady Bird Johnson 1912–2007: Memorial Tributes in the One Hundred Tenth Congress of the United States. S. Doc. No. 110-8. US Government Printing Office, 2008.

Goodwin, Doris Kearns. *Lyndon Johnson and the American Dream.* St. Martin's Griffin, 1976.

Johnson, Rebekah Baines. *A Family Album.* McGraw-Hill Book Company, 1965.

Johnson, Sam Houston. *My Brother Lyndon.* Cowles Book Company, 1969.

Middleton, Harry. *LBJ: The White House Years.* Harry N. Abrams, 1990.

Miller, Merle. *Lyndon: An Oral Biography.* G. P. Putnam's Sons, 1980.

Sinise, Jerry. *Lyndon Baines Johnson Remembered.* Eakin Publications, 1985.

Unger, Irwin, and Unger, Debi. *LBJ: A Life*. John Wiley and Sons, 1999.

Woods, Randall B. *LBJ: Architect of American Ambition*. Free Press, 2006.

www.ingramcontent.com/pod-product-compliance
Lightning Source LLC
Jackson TN
JSHW021256100426
100637JS00002B/11

* 9 7 8 1 4 7 7 3 3 2 1 4 6 *